WHAT ARE YOU DOING WITH GOD?

By Beth Thompson

For my children.

Table of Contents

Chapter 1

In your personal walk?

Have you ever asked yourself "What am I doing with God?' Most of us have not, because we do not like to think of how we are not using Him at all. We walk around with the Holy Spirit living inside of us and never let Him out. We do not let him work through us.

Some of us go through the motions as Christians and do not really do anything but go to church twice a week and that is it. We do not tell anybody about Jesus, we don't visit the sick, we don't invite others to church, we don't volunteer to help the poor, and most importantly, we don't have a relationship with God.

Everyone wants to put God in a box with a pretty bow and only bring Him out when it is convenient for us. We do not want to deal with our lack of relationship with Christ. God is forgiving, merciful, and loving. He is also jealous and angered when we do not obey Him and listen to His voice. We do not like to talk about the wrath of God, because then we must face up to our fears. Fear that we may not be what we are supposed to be.

Jesus is the Holy Son of God. Nobody wants to see Jesus as a human being and see that He was faced with the same things, you and I go through every day. We do not like to think about the fact that Jesus pooped in His diaper just like we did as a baby. We do not want to face the fact that Jesus got his hands and feet dirty, playing as a child. We do not like to think that Jesus bled like you and me when he got hurt. Jesus has all the same emotions you and I have. Usually we do not think about these things, because then we must see Him as a real person. Someone who can relate to our feelings, our thoughts, and our actions.

Jesus is Holy and should be revered as Holy, but we need to identify with Him as a person. How he reacted to his emotions is what is important. He is slow to anger, and when it came time to defend himself before Pilot, what did he do? He did not say anything. He let them pass judgement on him and let it go. He was accused of blasphemy against His father. He did not defend himself, because He knew His father better than anyone. God sees all and told us He is our vengeance, and He will be the judge of those who come up against us wrongfully. So, getting bent out of shape only causes us to be stressed and does not really hurt anyone but us. That does not mean we do not stand up for righteousness. When Jesus got angry in the temple, His anger was justified, because the people were using His father's temple as a marketplace, He had a righteous anger. God intended for His temple to be a Holy place of worship. So, we need to understand there are times that we need to stand up for what the word of God says is right. Keep in mind that we will be persecuted and disliked because we are Christians. It is important to understand the difference. Christ did not stand up to Pilot because Pilot did not understand the spiritual life of Jesus. Jesus had wisdom to know this, and He knew the sacrifice He was expected to give for us.

He was faced with temptation just like we are. The difference is how He chose to react to these things. He chose to rise above it all and be about His father's business. He was obedient to God and went about telling people about His father's commands. His will is that we would come to know and love Him, and to rely on Him for everything. Jesus came to show His father's love, mercy, and to warn us or the consequences of not following God's will. He came to give His life for us. (John 3:16) *16 For God so loved the world, that he gave His only begotten son, and whosoever believes in Him, shall not perish, but have eternal life.* He came to bring us life!

For us to get freedom from sin, we need to know what sin is. Sin means to cause offense of the laws, lawbreaker, disobedient, outright rejection of God's will, and evil committed against another.

(Exodus 20:2-17) This scripture reference is where the Ten Commandments can be found. They are not multiple choice; you do not get to choose which ones to follow as a child of God. These laws were set up for us to follow, to set us apart, for us to be able to recognize sin. God said He wants us to have One God—Him. It's alright to have hobbies, but when you are sitting in the house of God and your mind is on those hobbies, or whether you set the DVR to record your favorite show or what you are doing after church, then you are putting those things before Almighty God. It disrespects Him. He is a jealous God, he wants to first on your mind, especially when you are in the house of God. He said do not take my name in vain. What does that mean? It means that when you use His name in any other capacity, other than calling on Him in prayer, or praising or the authority to rebuke Satan, then it is in vain. (Hebrews 3:12-13) *12 Beware brethren, lest there be in any of you an evil heart of unbelief in departing from the Living God; 13 but exhort one another daily, while is called today, lest any of you be hardened through the deceitfulness of sin.* Unbelief is a grave sin because it leads us down a path to become stubborn and refuse to trust the truthfulness of God's word. When we sin and return to the world, it hardens our hearts and makes it easier to continue in that life of sin, we keep going back and forth between serving God and Satan. If you are not serving God, then you are serving Satan, plain and simple. Choose between the two and make a commitment and stick to it. We must be strong in the Lord to battle against Satan and begin to be able to birth gifts God has placed in each of us. You cannot grow your gifts, or follow the call on your life as long as you are trying to straddle the fence, because things get a little tough, or because you think God did not give you the answer you thought He should. You have to trust and understand everything has a season and a time and place, and if God gave it all to you at once, and you did not have to do any work, or go through trials, then you would not appreciate what He has done. You would have no reason to seek Him. No reason to pray, and no reason to trust and build your faith. How do we deepen our faith, it is through hard times, the storms, the trials, and the unanswered prayers, that we grow and become stronger in our relationship with God. He wants a relationship, not just for you to call on Him when you need something. He wants to walk with you and talk with you, and for you to prosper in all things, but you must seek Him daily. Prosperity comes in different forms and its not always monetary and wealth, fancy cars, houses etc. Prosperity comes from good health and having the necessities and living in the Joy of God. In verse 13 above we are exhorting one another, that means lift your brother and sister up, stay in contact with each other and pray for each other and be a watchman for one another's souls.

In Isaiah 6:1-13, Isaiah confessed he was unclean and was surrounded by a city of unclean people. He admitted that he

6

was a sinner, he was not giving God the praise and he was faced with, standing before God, and facing judgement and he was undone in his spirit. He was undone meaning he was at a loss as to what to say, what to do in that moment, but he just knew his life had come to an end. In this setting, we see the Seraphim were crying HOLY, HOLY, HOLY, but Isaiah was not praising God and he realized how unclean he really was in that moment. But God sent the Seraphim over to Isaiah and touched his lips with a live hot coal. The angel said your sin has been taken away and your sin is purged. The live coal represents the purification by the blood that would have been sacrificed at the altar and the fire of the Holy Spirit that enabled Isaiah to speak as a prophet. From this moment on the word of his mouth would be word of light and life, words from God to anyone who would listen. God told Isaiah to preach until nothing was left. God would have every right to take his grace from us. He could at any moment, and say that He is done, because of the rebellious nature we seem to continue to have. Turning deaf ears to what God has been trying to get us to understand. Keeping our eyes closed to our sin and our hearts become dull to His coming. God said WAKE UP! He wants people who will serve Him, really serve Him, and put away worldly things. Can you imagine being in Isaiah's shoes for a moment. To be faced with your life and be in the presence of God and just know that you are facing death. How awesome yet scary that must have been all at the same time. I mean to be in God's presence would be glorious and scary at the same time, because we know we aren't worthy to be in His holiness. To be faced with our sin and realize that our life has not been full of being a godly person. Isaiah was a prophet and he still felt unworthy. He still said he was undone. That is a moment that had to be a defining time for him. He saw his life defined and that God still would choose to offer him purification and a chance to go forth to preach and prophesy. In that moment God saw Isaiah as his chosen vessel, and he sent the angel to prepare him to receive his calling and purified his lips to carry the divine message of God. To preach until nothing was left. Isaiah spent his life preaching until all that needed to be said was said in his time for God's people.

A relationship with God starts with repentance. True repentance starts with believing in Jesus and asking God to forgive you of your sins, with a sincere heart. As you seek God and accept His love for you and receive Him into your heart and the sacrifice that Jesus made for all mankind. Jesus wants you to be free! Jesus wants us to be free from all the past mistakes, addictions, and wrong doings we have done, you will be free. He wants us to be free from the hurt that has been caused by others, who have dealt with us treacherously.

One thing to always remember that people do not always do the right thing, but God does. God will never fail you. He will always be faithful and meet our needs. People make mistakes because they usually put their own feelings first in any given situation. When we make a covenant with God and put Him first, and He will do the same in return. Because we have the gift of salvation, we can enter the Holy place with confidence by the blood of Jesus. If you have not really accepted Jesus and his grace, mercy, love, and forgiveness, then the time is now. You have an opportunity to accept Him by faith to let God lead you to a place where you can believe in the promises of His word. When you restore your relationship with God, you can restore other relationships through the love of

Jesus. We can approach God with boldness when we possess Christ's righteousness and not our own. We cannot count the sacrifice that Jesus made for us on the cross and shed his life's blood for us as a common everyday thing.

As Christians we put other people's feelings ahead of our own, we have less strife. That does not mean that we do not hold to God's truth and go against His word to spare feelings, but it does mean that we sacrifice our selfishness and love one another more than we love ourselves. Just like Christ did for us. He loved us more than He loved himself and He showed us that love on the cross, by laying down His life. He <u>chose</u> to die for us! What greater love is there than this? (Luke 4:18) [18] *The spirit of the Lord is upon me, because He has anointed me to preach the gospel to the poor; He has sent me to heal the brokenhearted, to proclaim liberty to the captives and recovery of sight to the blind, to set at liberty those who are oppressed.* Jesus was speaking about Himself, and His prophetic mission that He had come to fulfill. He fulfilled this scripture everywhere He went. He taught the people how to receive deliverance and how to repent of their sins. He healed them of their sickness of the physical body as well as the mind. He came to give liberty to those in captivity by the strongholds on their lives.

Strongholds come in many forms, such as sin, addictions, insecurities from our past. Maybe we have done someone wrong and do not feel like we can be forgiven or that we deserve forgiveness. The beauty of God's love is that even though we do not deserve forgiveness, He gives it freely anyway. He will forget our past transgressions and mistakes. His desire is that we would choose life, a life of eternity with Him, a life of service that honors Him as Lord of all. He will be true to His word. If we live by faith and do not draw back but continue in God's light and being diligent in the power of Jesus Christ who lives inside of you and me will help bring us to the throne of grace and forgiveness. (Matthew 4:17) *17 From that time Jesus began to preach. Repent for the kingdom of Heaven is at hand.* Let go of all the sin in your life. God is willing to forgive you. Some of us need to forgive God to have true repentance. God does not need our forgiveness, but when something horrible has happened in our life, that we do not understand why God allowed it to happen, then we become bitter towards God. The truth of the matter is, not everything that happens in our lives is God's fault. Sometimes we get ourselves in messes because we chose to get involved with the wrong relationship or chose to go away from God's statutes in His word. We get angry and do not want to accept responsibility for our own choices. There are circumstances that happen that are not our choice. There is evil in the world. Some people do evil things, because they are held by strongholds in their lives, in their past, or possessed by Satan's demons. When we hold onto anger against God for things that happened in our pasts, then we cannot be free from the grips that Satan has caused us to be chained by. We must let go of all the anger and then we can truly begin to live for Christ.

I would like to share my testimony; I had a lot of different abuse in my life. I have been emotionally, physically, and sexually abused. I had a lot of baggage that I was carrying around with me. I knew who God was and I knew Jesus had died on the cross for me, but I didn't have a relationship with Him because I was not free from all the pain that I had been through. I had been reading a book on healing and was driving down the road one morning and began to pray to God. As I was praying, I began to realize that through my prayer and pouring my heart out to God, I realized I was harboring anger against God. In the moments of weeping and praying I asked God to forgive me and I told him that I forgave Him too. That was my defining moment! I began to deal with my resentment and when I let go of the anger, I felt my heart open and it was almost like a closet, you know the one we push everything into when company's coming, yeah well my spiritual closet opened up and all the stuff I had crammed in there for years, came tumbling out. The Holy Spirit had been waiting a long time for me to let go! When I forgave God, I begin to experience Him in a way I never had before. I was able to be real with Him and have a relationship with Him. Because I had opened my heart, God was able to work in my life, because I had given my heart to Him. He gave us free will and He will not impose on that free will, but when I let go, God helped me to begin to heal. I needed to heal, before I could do anything that God had called me to do, I began to grow spiritually and began to discover the spiritual gifts, that I had an even more full life.

As we begin to let go and grow by reading the word of God, Satan will use tactics to attack our minds to cause us to fear, doubt, worry, and even try to reason out what God isn't doing, rather that what He is doing. Did He hear our prayers? Do not battle in your mind about the past. Once a person repents sincerely, the past sins that you committed are gone, forgotten, and will not be remembered anymore by God. (2 Thessalonians 2:1-2) [1] *Now brethren, concerning the coming of our Lord Jesus Christ and our gathering together to him, we ask you* [2] *not to be soon shaken in mind or troubled wither by spirit, by word, or by letter, as it from us, as though the day of Christ had come.* (Romans 7:23) [23] *But I see another law in my members warring against the law of my mind and bringing me into captivity to the law of sin, which is in my members.*

Satan tries to *remind* us of past sins, such as adultery, fornication, lying, cheating, stealing, pornography, sexual immorality, etc. Sin is darkness and Satan wants us to stay in darkness. When we give our hearts to God, we are brought out of darkness into the light. The light of God exposes sin. (Jeremiah 31:33-34) *33 But this is the covenant that I will make the house of Israel after those days, says the Lord; I will put my Law in their minds and write it on their hearts; and I will be their God and they shall be my people. 34No more shall every man teach his neighbor and every man his brother, saying ' Know the Lord', for they all shall know Me, from the least of them to the greatest of them, says the Lord. For I will forgive their iniquity (sin) and their sin I will remember no more.* When we come to Christ, our sin is forgiven. Satan tries to bring up the past, but the past is gone and to be given to God. God may choose to help you use your past for His glory, that someone else might come to know Him, but God will never use your past to torment you! Satan is the father of lies and would want to convince you that you are not forgiven and cannot be free. My friend that is a lie straight from the pits of Hell!

The second step to a relationship with Christ is to read His word and apply it to your life. We forget to put Jesus first. We need to spend time in his word because it strengthens our faith and helps us to face difficult times with a more positive attitude. Reading the Bible will convict us of our sins and help us to stay on the path of righteousness. As we read, we learn God's will for our lives. We find out truths about ourselves, that we did not even know existed. In your reading, you will find out God's ways, His laws to follow to obtain righteousness. We are counseled by reading the word of God. God's words are word of life and they speak to our hearts. Our hearts are circumcised and prepared for whatever purpose God has set before us. His word will give us answers to life's storms. The Holy Spirit will reveal God's truth and wisdom through reading the Bible. It is not called the Holy Bible for nothing.

Thirdly, we must have an open line of communication with God. We need to PRAY! (Colossians 4:2) ² *Devote yourselves to prayer, keeping alert in it with an attitude of thanksgiving.* It is okay to get real with God and it is okay to ask Him questions when you do not understand. In the old days we were taught not to ask God questions, but that is how His spirit teaches us His ways. He will reveal His answers to us. It is okay to tell Him we are angry and hurt. He will hear us and move on our behalf. You can tell Him your secrets and not worry about them getting out and everybody else knowing them. Go to God with your concerns, because when we go to others, they cannot fix it, and sometimes they cause more chaos than we need. We need to go to God first, before we try to tackle the problem. It may be something that he wants you to let him handle and he just wants you to trust him and allow him to fight the battle. There are situations that come in our lives that God wants to see how we handle them. To see if we will act as Jesus and allow God to build us up spiritually. Pray! By praying we open the door of our heart for the Holy Spirit to move and speak to us. As we intercede for others by faith, God will honor our requests and work on our behalf. By praying we are recognizing God as our creator. We recognize His power and His glory. We honor His wisdom and acknowledge in that wisdom that He knows what is best for us. Remember the prayer that never fails: God let your will be done in my life, in

Jesus name AMEN! Even when we do not know what to pray, this prayer will work, because we are completely trusting God to provide. (Proverbs3:5-6) *5 Trust in the Lord with all your heart and lean not to your own understanding. 6 In all your ways acknowledge Him, and He shall direct your paths.*

Going to church is the fourth way to increase your relationship with God. You will increase your faith and come to know Christ more intimately. There are several verses that encourage us to attend church. (Hebrews 10:25) *25 Not forsaking our assembling together, as the habit of some, but encouraging one another and all the more as you see the day drawing near.* This verse tells us to assemble to encourage one another and lift each other up to hold onto the promises of Christ's return. The Bible also tells us to hear the word of God to help increase our faith. (Romans 10:17) *17 So faith comes from hearing and hearing by the word of God.* We need to attend church to hear God's word preached to help us get a better understanding of His word as well being spiritually corrected when we need it, and be uplifted when we are going through storms in our lives.

There are responsibilities toward God. We all have a function as member in the body of Christ. (Romans 12:4-9) *4 Just as each of us has one body with many members, and these members do not all have the same function, 5 so we being many, are one body in Christ, and everyone members one of another. 6 We have different gifts, according to the grace given us. If a man's gift is prophesying, let him use it in proportion to his faith, 7 If it is serving, let him serve: if it is teaching; let him teach; 8 If it is encouraging, let him encourage; if its contributing to the needs of others, let him give generously; If it is leadership. Let him Govern diligently; if it is showing mercy, let him do it cheerfully. ⁹ Love must be sincere. Hate what is evil; cling to what is good.*

One of the responsibilities toward God is good stewardship. To be a good steward, we must be faithful over all that God has given us, serving others. Being content. He will not only bless us materially, but spiritually. He promised that we would not be able to hold it all. Stewardship also involves serving others and striving to be righteous in our lifestyle and not let sin defile us. We resemble in our behaviors that we belong to God and as such we are temples for the Holy Spirit. When Jesus sacrificed His life, He bought us with His blood. (1 Corinthians 6:19-20) *¹⁹Do you not know that your body is a temple of the Holy Spirit, who is in you, whom you have received from God? You are not your own. ²⁰ For you were bought at a price. Therefore, glorify God in your body and in your spirit, which are God's.* When we fail as good stewards we will be judged if we do not repent. We must glorify God in our actions, our bodies, our spirits. God gives us free will. In (Romans 1:18-32) we are told when we don't glorify God or try to change God into what we want him to be then our hearts become corrupt and we will be judged for our poor stewardship and be sentenced according to God's will. *¹⁸ For the wrath of God is revealed from Heaven against all ungodliness and unrighteousness of men, who suppress the truth in unrighteousness. ¹⁹ because what may be known of God is manifest in them, for God has shown it to them. ²⁰ For since the creation of the world, His invisible attributes are clearly seen, being understood by the things that are made even His eternal power and Godhead, so that they are without excuse. ²¹ because, although they knew God, they did not glorify Him as God, nor were thankful, but became futile in their thoughts and their foolish hearts were darkened. [22] Professing to be wise, they became fools, [23] and changed the glory of the incorruptible God into an image made like corruptible man and birds and four-footed animals and creeping things. [24] Therefore God also gave them up to uncleanness, in the lusts of their hearts, to dishonor their bodies among themselves, [25] who exchanged the truth of God for the lie, and worshiped and served the creature rather that the Creator, who is blessed forever. Amen. [26] For this reason God gave them up in vile passions. For even their women exchanged the natural use for what is against nature. [27] Likewise also men, leaving the natural use for what is against nature, burned in their lust for one another, men with men committing what is shameful, and receiving to themselves the penalty of their error which is due. [28] And even as they did not like to retain God in their knowledge, God gave them up over to a debased mind, to do those things which are not fitting. [29] being filled with all unrighteousness; sexual immorality, wickedness, maliciousness, full of envy, murder, strife, deceit, and evil mindedness; they are whisperers. [30] backbiters, haters of God, violent, proud, boasters, inventors of evil things, disobedient to parents, [31]undiscerning, untrustworthy, unloving, unforgiving, unmerciful; [32] who, knowing the righteous judgment of, that those who practice such things are deserving of, not only do the same but also approve of those who practice them.* God's character is Holy and disapproves of sin, but if we seek to repent and know His ways, He will be faithful to his good stewards.

Another responsibility to God is tithing (Malachi 3:10) 10 *Bring all tithes into the storehouse, that there may be food in My house, and try me now in this; says the Lord of Hosts. If I will not open the windows of Heaven and pour out for you such blessings that there will not be room enough to receive it.* If we are faithful in our tithes, God will open the windows of Heaven. He will not only bless us materially, but spiritually. He promised that we would not be able to hold it all. Tithing is a commandment by God. It is about obedience and about honoring the covenant we made with God. It is about making a sacrifice to God. It is about setting a standard as Christians for others to follow that shows character traits of honesty, and integrity. When we tithe, we recognize God as Lord and creator of all. We give back to Him for all that He has given to us. He gave us life!

Chapter 2

At Home?

So many times, we get home from work and sigh with relief, because now we can be ourselves. Then all the grumbling comes. Grumbling about our jobs, our spouses, our children. Oftentimes we do not even realize the belittling things that come out of our mouths. We just find something to home in on and let loose.

At work we put on a different face because there is no way we would treat our co-worker that way. I mean we must work with them everyday and we want to keep the lines of communication open. But we hurt the ones at home the most. They put up with all our faults because they love us, and we know our co-workers will not. At home we feel less pressured and can count on our family to stick by us. And we sometimes get fooled into believing we do not have anything to lose at home, but we have more and should be aware of the way we behave to the ones who we count on the most.

Husbands and Wives, you must, love and respect one another more than your friends, your co-workers, your boss, and your family. They will be the ones there to take care of you when you can no longer do it yourself. (Ephesians 5:33) *33 Nevertheless let every one of you so love his wife as himself, and the wife reverence her husband.* (Proverbs 12:4) *4 An excellent wife is the crown of her husband.* God expects us to treat our spouses with great respect. When there is strife between you and your spouse, then your spirit is bound, and those burdens become a stronghold on your life and hinder you from being spiritually free. (1Peter3:7-8) *7 You husbands likewise, live with your wives in a understanding way, as with a weaker vessel, since she is a woman, and grant her honor as a fellow heir of the grace of life, so the your prayers may not be hindered. [8] To sum it up, let all harmonious, sympathetic, brotherly, kindhearted, and humble in spirit.* Let us face it, men treat themselves with respect and they do it with pride. That's great! Men should take care of themselves. They should look good for their wives. They should try to look at themselves through their wife's eyes and why she fell in love with them and try to maintain that image. Yes, we grow and change over the years as we gain more wisdom, but the husband should represent himself in a way that is pleasing to God and his spouse.

Husbands your wife need you to listen, <u>really listen!</u> They do not necessarily want you to solve their problems, just listen to them. A woman needs affection and intimacy. She needs to be told that she is beautiful and made to feel cherished like a fine jewel. She needs you to talk to her with details. She needs you to share your dreams. Women are a gift given by God to be nurturing and loving. Men let them be what God created them to be. It is an instinct that should not be taken lightly. Husbands, you need to support your wife's dreams. Women are not weak in the sense that they do not have their own thoughts or wisdom. God expected women to look to the husband for strength to care for them and protect them. The man is supposed to care for her as though she is precious, not treat her like she is beneath him, but as a partner that is an essential part of him. A part that is softer and equals out the hard side of the man. Where the man is strong, the woman is nurturing. (Ephesians 5:25,28-31) *[25] Husbands, love your wives, just as Christ also loved the church and gave himself up for her. [28] So husband's ought to also love their own wives as they love their own bodies. He who loves his own wife loves himself;* [29] *for no one ever hated his own flesh, nourishes, and cherishes it, just as Christ also does the church.* [30] *because we are member of His body.* [31] *For this cause a man shall leave his father and mother and cleave to his wife and the two shall become one flesh.*

Wives also have a certain responsibility to their husbands. (Colossians 3:18-19) [18] *Wives, submit yourselves unto, as it is fit in the Lord.* [19] *Husbands love your wives and not be bitter against them.* Wives your husbands need to feel important. They need for you to feed their ego. Tell your husband that he is handsome. Men need affection and intimacy. They need time alone and to get in touch with their strength and their purpose as the protector and provider for their families. Encourage your husband's dreams and stand by him when he fails. (Ephesians 5:22-24) [22] *Wives be subjected to your own husbands, as to the Lord.* [23] *For the husband it the head of the wife, as Christ is the head of the church. He as himself being savior of the body.* [24] *But as the church is subject to Christ, so also the wives ought to be to their husbands in everything.* Wives you should support your husband's decisions and should be a helpmate and respect him. That is what these verses are telling us. A woman should be a virtuous woman. (see Proverbs 31). Proverbs 31 is a process for some of us while others seem to become virtuous more easily. I pray all the time to reach for the goal of a more virtuous woman.

Both spouses need to remember they belong to each other. Because you are one flesh, and spirit, you belong to one another. You do not own your own body. Both of you should not withhold from one another. God's word warns against husbands and wives withholding sexual intimacy from one another. We need to be in tune with each other and when we connect intimately, the bonds are made stronger and it is harder for Satan to divide what is strong. Keeping God and His word ever present in our marriages will help it to withstand the test of time. (1Corithians 7:2-5) *² Nevertheless, because of sexual immorality; Let each man have his own wife, and let each wife have her own husband. ³ Let the husband render to his wife affection due her and likewise also the wife to her husband. ⁴ The wife does not have authority over her own body, the husband does, and likewise the husband does not have authority over his own body, the wife does. ⁵ Do not deprive one another except with consent for a time, that you may give yourselves to fasting and prayer, and come together again so that Satan does not tempt you because of your lack of self-control.*

The word advises us to be equally yoked (both be believers in Christ). The reason for this, is to protect against strife in their marriage, but the word does give instruction about being unequally yoked. (see 1 Corinthians 7:12-16) If we are married and one spouse becomes a believer, and the other is not, it is okay to remain together. The verses referenced in 1 Corinthians 7:12-16, tells us that when one spouse is saved and the other is not, the one that is sanctifies the unsaved one. We cannot force our spouse to become saved, but we can live the example of Christ in our lives so that they may become saved. If harmony can be achieved there is no reason to leave.

Children also need to feel safe and know that they can trust you to help them to be well adjusted Christians. They will learn by the example you set. If they see you go to church and be all smiles and at home an ogre, then what are they really learning? The ten commandments tell us to honor our father and mother, but how can your children do this if we don't' give them something to honor?

Our children need to know that when they make a mistake or disappoint us with their actions, that we will handle the situation in a Godly way. This will build the foundation of trust. Trust is important between a child and parent. Every parent's dream is that their teens would talk to them about what is going on in their lives. How can they talk to us it we fly off the handle every time they stumble? That does not mean that we cannot get mad, but how we handle the anger is what is important. (Colossians 3:21) [21] *Fathers, provoke not your children, lest they be discouraged.* Now this does not mean let your children have free reign, but to talk to our children in a way that will help them with their spiritual growth and not damage their self-confidence. (Proverbs 22:6) [6] *Train up a child in the way he should go, and when he is old, he will not depart from it.* If your child should turn away from their walk with God, do not fret. Keep trusting God because God's word does not go void. Teach your children to obey the word of God. Teach them that the people they hang out with will reflect who they are. Teach them to be careful to uphold all appearances of being a Christian when they are around non-Christians, so they make Godly choices. Teach them to be an example that their friends can respect and look up to them and be the example they set; their friends will learn of Christ.

The home is where the love begins, and it is where the support system is founded. To keep that support, there must be respect, understanding, and prayer. To give an example, my husband, and our son will pray together for our loved ones, especially when there is a need. We unite in God and in our faith and God strengthens the bond. (Matthew 18:20) [20] *For where two or three gathered in my name, I am in the midst of them.* Stand on this promise and let God in and He will keep the lines of communication open.

When a man and a woman fall in love, they would give their life for one another. When a mother gives birth to a child, she would lay her life down for that child to protect it. We were given this unconditional love by God. How is it that we cannot love God the same way? Why is it that we have so much trouble comprehending that Jesus loves us so much so, that He gave His life for us? He believes in us. He loves us with that unconditional love. He will go to the ends of the earth with us. He will never leave us. He will be there in the good and bad times. (Psalms 139:1-24). *1 O Lord You have searched me and known me. 2 You know my sitting down and my rising up; You understand my thoughts afar off. 3 You comprehend my path and my lying down and are acquainted with all my ways. 4 For there is not a word on my tongue, but behold, O Lord, you know altogether. 5 You have hedged me behind and before and laid your hand upon me. 6 Such knowledge is too wonderful for me; It is high, I cannot attain it. 7 Where can I go from your Spirit? Or where can I flee your presence? 8 If I ascend into Heaven, you are there, if I make my bed in Hell, behold, you are there. 9 If I take the wings of the morning, and dwell in the uttermost parts of the sea, 10 Even there Your hand shall lead me, and Your right hand shall hold me. 11 If I say, "surely the darkness shall fall on me," Even the night shall be light about me; 12 Indeed, the darkness shall not hide from you, but the night shines as the day; the darkness and the light are both alike to you. 13 For you formed my inward parts; You covered me in my mother's womb. 14 I will praise You, for I am fearfully and wonderfully made; marvelous are Your works, and that my soul knows very well. 15 My frame was not hidden from You, when I was made in secret, and skillfully wrought in the lowest parts of the earth. 16 Your eyes saw my substance, being yet unformed. And as in your book, they all were written, the days fashioned for me, when it was yet there were none of them. ¹⁷ How precious also are your thoughts to me, O God. How great is the sum of them? ¹⁸ if I should count them, they would be more in number than the sand; When I awake, I am still with You. ¹⁹ Oh that you would slay the wicked, O God! Depart from me, therefore you bloodthirsty men. ²⁰ For they speak against you wickedly; Your enemies take your name in vain. ²¹ Do I not hate them, O Lord, who hate you? And am not I grieved with those that rise up against thee? ²² I hate them with perfect hatred; I count them my enemies. ²³ Search me O God and know my heart; try me and know my anxieties; ²⁴ And see if there is any wicked way in me and lead me in the way of everlasting.*

God knows our thoughts and our hearts, and He sees the truth that lies there and in our thoughts. We need to become intimate with the Father and treat Him like we do the people in our lives that we love so that we would die for. If we trust Him above all then He will take care of the rest. (Matthew 28:20b) *²⁰ I command you; I am with you always even to the ends of the age.* (Hebrews 3:5-6) *⁵ Let your character be free from the love of money, being content, with what you have; for He himself has said. "The Lord is my helper; I will not be afraid. What shall a man do to me?"*

God has blessed you with the family, material things you have, He blessed you with every talent and skill you have. He gave us these things because he wants us to look to Him as the creator that He is. He wants us to love Him and give Him praise even when we cannot see the good in any given situation. We must have an intimate relationship with God to hear His voice, when He speaks to us, so that we can be obedient to His commands.

Do not take family for granted. Be thankful always for they are a blessing from God. If we do not love and respect one another in our families, then how can we show others the love of Christ?

When we let God enter our home, changes occur. Satan becomes angry. He will try to cause strife and test us to make us waiver in our faith. Praise God during those trials. Satan will bring up your past mistakes to make you feel ashamed. The following verse tells us to rejoice in trials, because God will be faithful, as we will be faithful and trust Him. Remember with trials, comes blessings. (1Peter 4:12-19)

[12] Beloved so not be surprised at the fiery ordeal among you. Which comes upon you for testing, as though some strange thing were happening to you. [13] but to the degree that you share the sufferings of Christ, keep on rejoicings; so that also at the revelation of His glory, you may rejoice with exultation. [14] If you are reviled for the name of Christ, you are blessed, because the Spirit of glory and of God rests upon you. [15] By no means let any of you suffer as a murderer, or thief, or evildoer, or troublesome meddler; [16] but in that anyone suffers as a Christian, let him not feel ashamed. But in that name let him glorify God. [17] For it is time for judgment to begin with the household of God; and it begins with us first, what will be the outcome for those who do not obey the gospel of God? [18] And if it is with difficulty that the righteous is saved, what will become of the Godless and the sinner? [19] Therefore, let those also who suffer according to the will of God entrust their souls to a faithful creator in doing what is right. If we put Him above all in our lives, then we can truly be free in our salvation.

Chapter 3

In Your Job?

In our daily walk with God, we are watched closely. The slightest misstep and we are fallen Christians. We have back slid. So, what do we do with God at work? Do we engage in idle gossip about other employees? The devil is sly, and he will use every tool in his bag to cause us to fall into his trap and use it against us? The Bible calls a gossiper a tale bearer and warns against gossiping. (Leviticus 19:16) *16 You shall not go about as a talebearer among your people; nor shall you take a stand against the life of your neighbor; I am the Lord.*

The Bible also warns against associating with those who participated in gossip. (Proverbs 20:19) *19 He who goes as a talebearer reveals secrets; Therefore, do not associate with one who flatters with his lips.* A lot of the times when we engage in gossip, then it's turned around and used against us, and before you know it you were the one who started the whole process and the guilty walks away as though they are innocent, and you are having to repair the damage.

A place of employment is the hardest place to function as a Christian, especially when you are surrounded by non-believers. Non – Christians have this misconception, that when a person decides to follow Christ, that person becomes perfect. The reality is when a person becomes a Christian, they strive to be as much like Christ as possible. The difference between and Christian and non-Christian is when a Christian sins, they feel convicted and repent to God, and when a non-Christian sins, they do not feel the same guilt, because the have not invited the Spirit of God into their hearts to reveal the truth of any wrong doing and continue in their sin. . They are not aware because they do not; understand the ways of the Holy Spirit, because they are not walking by the Spirit. A Christian must be careful. Some jobs will terminate your employment if you discuss religion at all. So, what do you do if you feel led by God to witness to another employee? You must follow God's lead and trust him.

The way we conduct ourselves at work is one of the true tell-tale signs of our Christianity. If we walk in the light of Jesus, then all other things die. Carrying the joy of Christ in your heart, will be contagious and others will want to gain this same joy in their lives.

If you are behaving the way Christ would behave toward your fellow co-workers, then they will want to do things for you and do not even know why. The Holy Spirit is so powerful that it will affect those around you, and they will not be able to help themselves. (Romans 8 :5-8) 5 *For those who live according to the flesh, set their minds on the things of the flesh, but those who live according to the spirit, the things of the spirit.* [6] *For to be carnally minded is death, but to be spiritually minded is life and peace.* [7] *Because the carnal mind is enmity against God; for it is subject to the law of God, nor indeed can be.* [8] *So then, those who are in the flesh cannot please God.*

Christians must walk in the Spirit, speak in Spirit, and act in Spirit. One cannot do God's bidding when he starts putting his own thoughts into what he has been called to do. God sent the Holy Spirit to comfort us and give us guidance and strength to ward off the ways of the world. When we are in situations that are not of God why do we find it hard to walk away? Everybody wants to be accepted but what is more important? Is it more important to be accepted by your peers and gain a moment of pleasure, or to accepted by God and have eternal life? This is the area in which we fail most of the times as

Christians. We must crucify the flesh daily and renew our covenant with God. (Galatians 5:24-26) *24 Now those who belong to Christ Jesus have crucified the flesh with its passions and desires. 25 If we live by the Spirit, let us also walk by the Spirit. 26 Let us not become boastful, challenging one another, envying one another.*

To keep our eyes on the light of Jesus, is the only way to show others the path to Heaven. How do we do this? Some would say pull out your Bible and start reading them verses of salvation. This may work for some; but others need to be led more gently and then you can direct them to the word of God. They need to see Jesus in us first. Seed must be planted and when the time is right, you will be able to take the Bible and show them the truth. They must be ready to receive God's word before you can show them.

Jesus said to love one another. If we truly let Jesus shine through is and show one another love even when we may disagree, we will show them the true way to God. God will work through you if you let him. When encountered with a co-worker that looks alone and sad, give a word of encouragement. Tell them that you are praying for them. You do not have to know the details of what they are going through to pray for them, because God already knows. Just show them you love them. By showing them love, you show them God's love.

Another way to lead someone to Christ, is showing them your way of life. Showing the joy of Christ, even we aren't having the best day. Every morning go to work and greet your co-workers. Sometimes you will be met with a grumble, and sometimes be met with a smiling face. If you have joy in your attitude, it will be catching and others will feel better too, for having been around you and the Holy Spirit that lives inside of you. They will ask you how you stay so happy, and then comes the opportunity to tell them it is so much more than mere happiness. It is a joy that carries you through and gives you the strength in knowing that your hope lies in Christ. Happiness fades. Joy is coming from a deeper place that can only come form God. Use the opportunity to tell them about God's love and the joy that he has given you through the knowledge of salvation and Christ's sacrifice. Try it! God will show you the rest.

There are times that people have to see it for themselves and these people are the people you have to direct to God's word and show them what is says about being a sinner and what we must do to go to Heaven. Just be sensitive to the Holy Spirit and give them time to digest what you have shared with them and then come back to it if you get the sense they are not receiving the truth of God's plan for their life. When they are digesting what has been shown to them, they will begin to have questions and then they will come back to you and look for more answers. They will come back to you, because they will trust you to tell them the truth and if you do not have the answers, do not pretend that you do. Tell them let me research it and get back to you or let me call my Pastor. They will respect you more for admitting that you don't have it all figured out. When you plant a seed, it has to take root, and then when the seed begins to break open, it will sprout. That tiny sprout will need to be watered and they will want the water from you. You will be able to add to and throw a little fertilizer on too. They will begin to want more and before you know it, they will bloom right before your eyes with Christ's love shining through. They will have blossomed into a believer and be ready to accept Jesus into their lives and then they will experience an abundant life.

Chapter 4

At Church?

The gifts that have been given to us by God are given for His will. These gifts are not to be taken for granted, not to be envied, but to be set apart and protected. They are to be used for the Glory of God. When the body of Christ comes together, and those gifts are combined, the gifts of the body complement one another and can be used effectively to increase the Kingdom of God. It would be God's will that not one be lost, not one perishes, but all be saved. Once the body of Christ begins to grasp this concept of walking in the spirit and individual anointing, then we can truly walk-in righteousness. We can be men, women, and children that have purposed in their hearts to seek God's heart. Seeking God's heart (will for our lives) will make our lives a life worth dying for. That Jesus' sacrifice is not in vain.

(1Corinthians 12:3-13) *3 Wherefore I give you to understand, that no man speaking by the Spirit of God calleth Jesus accursed; and that no man can say that Jesus is Lord, but by the Holy Ghost. 4 Now there are diversities of gifts, but the same Spirit. 5 And there are differences of administrations, but the same Lord. 6 And there are varieties of effects, but the same God who works in all things in all persons. 7 But to each one is given the manifestation of the Spirit of the common good. 8 For to one is given the word of wisdom through the Spirit and to another the word of knowledge according to the same Spirit, 9 to another faith by the same Spirit, and to another gifts of healing by the one Spirit, 10 and to another the effecting of miracles, and to another prophecy, and to another the distinguishing of Spirits, to another various kinds of tongues and to another the interpretation of tongues. [11] But to one and the same Spirit, works all these things, distributing to each one individually just as He wills. [12] For even as the body is one and yet has many members, and all the members of the body, though they are many, are one body, so also is Christ. [13] For by one Spirit we were all baptized into one body, whether slaves or free, and we were made to drink of one Spirit.*

God is tired of all the bickering between Christians, the problem is no one can get along outside their denomination. Christians talk about fixing the world, but Christians need to be fixed first. Arguing scriptures, arguing beliefs, and tearing each other down in the process is not what God has called us to do as His bride.

(Romans 15:6-7) *[6] That ye may be one mind and one mouth glorify God, even the father of our Lord Jesus Christ. [7] Wherefore ye receive on another as Christ also received us to the glory of God. (1 Corinthians 1:9-10) [9] God is faithful, by whom ye were called unto the fellowship of His son Jesus Christ, [10] Now I beseech you, brethren by the name of our Lord Jesus Christ, that ye all speak the same thing; and there are no divisions among you; but ye be perfectly joined together in the same mind, and in the same judgment.* Christians do not glorify God when they disagree with one another about differences in their denominations. As these verses stated, Christians need to band together and unite in God to make non-believers realize the type of life they are missing. According to the dictionary, unite means to join into one group or entity. Entity means one that exists. Christians are alive and so is Jesus. So, Jesus lives in each of us, and we must show others His light that dwells within us. If we constantly go around tearing each other's denomination down, we do not edify our brothers and sisters in

Christ. Therefore, we are not united. When you are alone it is harder to accomplish a task at hand. But when you are united, with many, the task is much easier to tackle. That is why there are groups today that are causing Christianity to become a minority in the world. That is why people are influenced by religions that do not represent Christianity or its values. We have groups in the world that are changing the constitution, they are changing what is allowed to be preached, and what venue it can be preached and they have been successful in taking God out of many public forums. Meanwhile Christians are arguing over issues that are distracting us from the real problems that we should be tackling as the body of Christ. The enemy is hard at work people! Christians need to get it together and start binding together in Spirit and in truth and start standing up for what is right and taking back what the enemy has been successful in stealing from us. We need to fight to keep God in our constitution, our children's schools, and public forums. It is time to step up to the plate! (Philippians 2:1-5) *¹ If therefore there is any encouragement in Christ, if there is any consolation of love, if there is any fellowship of the Spirit, if any affection and compassion, ² make my joy complete by being of the same mind, maintaining the same love, united in Spirit intent on one purpose. ³ Do nothing from selfishness or empty conceit, but with humility of mind, let each of you regard one another as more important than himself. ⁴ Do not merely look out for your own personal interest, but the interest of others. ⁵ Have this attitude in yourselves which is also in Christ Jesus.* When someone attacks your religion, do not let Satan steal your joy, pray for the person that attacks you and read God's word and let His voice speak to you. Listen to what **He Says and** apply it to your life. Remember God cannot lie. His word says so. (Titus 1:2) *² In hope of eternal life which God, who cannot* *lie, promised before time began.* The Holy Spirit will speak truth to your soul. We have been called to do good works, but these works are not what gets us to Heaven. God promised a place in Heaven by grace that came with His son Jesus, who died for our sins. By His blood, our hearts and souls are cleansed, and we are made heirs to everlasting life. (Titus 3:5-8) *⁵ Not by works of righteousness which we have done, according to His mercy, He saved us, through the washing of regeneration and renewing of the Holy Spirit. ⁶ Whom He poured out on us abundantly through Jesus Christ. ⁷ that having been justified by His grace we should become heirs to the hope of eternal life. ⁸ This is a faithful saying and these things I want you to affirm constantly, that those who have believed in God should be careful to maintain good works. These things are good and profitable to men.* (I suggest reading the whole book of Titus) Good works will not get you to into Heaven but, we should maintain good works, which is through charity to others. We do it to glorify God, not to bring glory to ourselves. We give generously because God has given so generously to us. We share the blessings of God. Faith without good works is dead. This meaning that because of our faith, we do good works by helping in time of need and that God receives the glory for it through it.

When you are attacked stand up for what you believe in (but do not become the attacker by tearing any one down in the process) and do not become double minded. This is not of God. Do not fear because God will be there with you. You cannot speak on things and believe another. You cannot deny what God has spoken in your heart and go along with what someone else says to be accepted. We should not be fighting. We should be working together to increase the Kingdom of God. We should be loving one another. Jesus did not tell us to take scripture and tear each other apart. He gave us the word to learn His will for our lives and to be able to share His love with those who do not know of His goodness. For instance, if someone asks you about homosexuality, (Leviticus 20:13), tell them what God's word says about it. You can do this without arguing. Tell them the truth and, they will have to decide for themselves if they accept it. You cannot force the truth on someone. God wants us to edify our brothers and sisters in Christ. God expects us to correct them with love and gentleness, when they stray away from the faith, to help them to come back to their faith. Sometimes just showing love will speak more volumes than any words we say out loud. We must love everyone, even if we do not agree with their life choices. We love them and treat them the way Jesus would. We must control our tongue through faith in God. The tongue has the power to strengthen or break a person. We have the power to speak things into people's lives that can help or destroy them. (James 3:5-12) *5 Even so the tongue is a little member and boasts great things, See how great a forest, a little fire kindles! 6 and the tongue is a fire; a world of iniquity (sin). The tongue is so set among our members that it defiles the whole body and sets on fire the course of nature: and it is set on fire by Hell. 7 For every kind of beast or bird, or reptile, and creature of the sea, is tamed by mankind. 8 But no man can tame the tongue. It is unruly evil, full of deadly poison. 9 With it we bless our God, and Father, and with it we curse men, who have been made in similitude (likeness) of God. 10 Out of the same mouth proceed blessing and cursing. My brethren, these things ought not to be so. 11 Does a spring send forth fresh water and bitter from the same opening? 12 Can a fig tree, my brethren, bear olives, or a grapevine bear figs? Thus, no spring yields both salt and fresh.* The book of James is a great book in the Bible! It teaches us how we must always be careful in what we say and act. We must always be doing the work of God. We cannot give in to idle worldly things and say evil things and then say blessings. Satan is tricky and will sneak things in on us from time to time and cause us to be snared by our own words. We are flesh and live in the world, but we cannot let the world live in us, if we want God to dwell there. We must stay in His word daily. We must ask for the Holy Spirit to be renewed daily in our lives and we must not say anything that is not of God. If you say it then you give Satan ammunition to use against you, and before you know it, you have really acted in an ungodly way. There is good news! God loves us despite our flesh and will continue to remove the worldly ways from our lives if we submit and give Him free will over our lives.

Fixing the problems in the world would be easier to face up to if we unite against Satan. Satan tries to use us to tear each other down. He will creep into our minds and tell us we are better that our Christians brothers and sisters, Once we start to believe the lies that we are better or that our religion is better, we began to separate ourselves form the unity of Christ has instilled in us with the Holy Spirit. Though there are churches that have begun to pull together and I believe we will see more in our time on earth. You are needed to help accomplish this unification of saints!

Christ called us to witness to others, Jesus wants us to lead non-believers to Him. He wants to give them the keys to Heaven. A lot of us know the keys, but do we use them? Jesus wants us to give them the plan of salvation. He will do the work in their hearts to transform them into His new creation. He will place them where He wants them and set them up in a place that they will be able to perform the ministry work He has planned for them. The trouble Christians run into; is they want to put their own opinions into the salvation plan. To be a good witness, as a Christian, share what God has done for you. Tell them how when you read the scriptures, how it impacts you and how it makes you want to be better and how your soul feels alive. Offer encouragement to them to have the same opportunity to accept the gift of salvation and let them know that life's answers are in God's word. You have an opportunity to help them understand the Bible with the help of the Holy Spirit. We must work by the Spirit and not in our own flesh. (Philippians 1:27) *27 Only let your conversations be as is becometh the gospel of Christ, that whether I come and see you, or else be present, be absent, I may hear of your affairs, that you stand in one Spirit, with one mind striving for the faith of the gospel.*

We, the body of Christ need to reach out to one another and stand firm against the world. We must not loose focus on our duties as told by the Bible. (See John 15:12). Jesus said to love one another as I have loved you.

Chapter 5

As a nation?

(Isaiah 26:17-18) *[17]Like as a woman with child, that draweth near the time of her delivery, is in pain, and cried out in the pangs; so, we have been in thy sight O Lord. [18] We have been with child, we have been in pain, we have as it were brought forth wind; we have not wrought any deliverance in the earth; neither have the inhabitants of the world fallen.* The troubles we face are important to the growing process and we are spiritually pregnant with a bounty of God's word. We can bring forth word to birth deliverance for God's kingdom. Are we birthing the right things, such as, love, peace, and joy? Or are we birthing discord violence and giving into the world?

In todays society- Violence, drugs, and vulgarity has become a way of life. We live today in a nation that is agreeable to gay marriage, agreeable to let prayer be taken out of school, and every biblical principle that this country was founded upon, be snatched away. We need God in the world now more than ever. Christians must unite and stand up, and be heard, for we can make a difference, if only we lay our own differences aside. If we put the Spirit of God first and let all the rest fall away, then we will be one step closer to being Christ-like.

Homosexuality is an abomination to the Lord. (Leviticus 18:22-23) *[22] You shall not lie with a male as a with a woman. It is an abomination. [23] Nor shall you mate with any animal, to defile yourself with it. Nor shall any woman stand before and animal to mate with it. It is a perversion.* God is noticeably clear on His feelings on this issue.

Prayer has been left out of our schools and is the reason that violence and vulgarity have become second nature to our children. (1Thessalonians 5:16-22) *16 Rejoice always. 17 Pray without ceasing. 18 In everything gives thanks for this is the will of God in Christ Jesus for you. 19 Do not quench the Spirit. 20 Do not despise prophecies. 21 Test all things: hold fast to what is good. 22 Abstain from every form of evil.* The Bibles says every form of evil. Prayer and studying the Bible are the very substances every Christian needs to stay in touch with God.

Pornography, drugs, and violence has taken over the television and infected the minds of the people and caused them to lust after fleshly desires, that God warned us about in His word. I am not against watching television, just that we should be careful of what we watch. We can see in God's word to abstain from lust. (Ezekiel 23:14-17) *14 But she increased her harlotry; She looked at men portrayed on the wall; images of Chaldeans portrayed in vermillion. 15 Girded with belts around their waist, flowing turbans on their head, all of them looking like captains, in the manner of the Babylonians of Chaldea, the land of their nativity. 16 As soon as her eyes saw them, she lusted for them and sent messengers to them in Chaldea. 17 Then the Babylonians came to her, into the bed of love, and they defiled her with immorality; so, she was defiled by them and alienated herself from them.* Ezekiel 23 is talking about two sisters and they were corrupt in their lust and harlotry, and Ezekiel was warning against the judgement that will follow this kind of behavior. We indulge into physical desires beyond the bounds of marriage and we are falling into sin. When we fall into sin and we war against our own soul and are defiling ourselves and not upholding the principles of God. (1 Peter 2:11) *11 Beloved, I beg you as sojourners and pilgrims, abstain from fleshly lust which war against the soul.*

If we delve into the desires of alcohol and drugs, we bring ourselves into spiritual bondage. When we delve into these desires, we find ourselves addicted and bound by them. We struggle to make sense of it all and we have trouble breaking the chains and become captive by our own minds, that keep us from seeking freedom. People tell themselves that they cannot be loved or forgiven, because not only did they defile their bodies, they committed crimes or hurt others in the process of their addictions and find it hard to break the cycle of guilt. They cannot do it on their own, but God can help them gain deliverance. He will be a lifeline to deliverance and break the cycle of pain and gain their life back and be restored to their families. You can be a temporary lifeline through prayer and being that constant to intercede for them and not giving up on the promises of God that they can be saved. (Proverbs 20:1) tells us alcohol will lead us astray and it is not wise, because it causes us to become brawlers and not ourselves. The body is a temple and when the temple is filled with Jesus, He makes it Holy. We must consciously be aware that we are a vessel that God wants to use for His glory. That His kingdom may be increased, and others may see Him represented in our lives. (I Corinthians 6:19-20) [19] *Or do you not know that your body is the temple of the Holy Spirit, who is in you, whom you have from God, and you are not your own.* [20] *For you were bought at a price; therefore, glorify God in your body and in your spirit, which are God's.* Anything that would cause the body or the soul harm, are things we need to be careful of. Drugs, alcohol, pornography, and homosexuality are practices that can destroy our bodies and harm our minds and soul. They destroy us by keeping us from enjoying life naturally, the way God intended. He intended that we find Joy, peace, and true happiness in Him, by worshipping and loving Him as He loves us. We can find

Strength we need in Him, by staying connected to Him through His word, prayer, and contact with fellow believers to break away from those things that once controlled us.

(Genesis 9:8-17) *8 Then God spoke to Noah and to his sons with him, saying 9And as for Me, behold, I establish My covenant with you and your descendants after you. 10 and with every living creature that is with you, the birds, the cattle, and every beast of the earth. 11 Thus I establish My covenant with you; Never again shall all flesh be cut off by the waters of the flood; never again shall there be a flood to destroy the earth. 12 And God said: This is a sign of the covenant which I make between Me and you, and every living creature that is with you, for perpetual generations: 13 I set My rainbow in the cloud., and is shall be for the sign of the covenant between Me and the earth. 14 It shall be, when I bring a cloud over the earth, that the rainbow shall be seen in the cloud:; 15 and I will remember My covenant which is between Me and you and every living creature of all flesh; the waters shall never again become a flood to destroy all flesh. 16 The rainbow shall be in the cloud, and I will look on it to remember the everlasting covenant between God and every living creature of all flesh that is on earth. 17 And God said to Noah. "This is the sign of the covenant which I have established between Me and all flesh of the earth".* God established His covenant with Noah after the flood, God made a promise never to destroy the earth again by water and the rainbow is the promise. God's covenant is binding and is a part of His character to be true to His word and uphold truth in His dealings with us. He will be honest and faithful. He promised that He would not destroy the earth by flooding again.

(Genesis 12:1-3) *1 Now the Lord said to Abram: "Get out of your country, from your family and from you father's house, to a land that I will show you. ² I will make you a great nation; I will bless you and make your name great, and you shall be a blessing. ³ I will bless those who bless you, and I will curse him, who curses you; and in you, all the families of the earth shall be blessed.*" God established Abraham as the father of all nations, and He made a covenant to make him a father. God made seven promises to Abraham in this passage.

1)   God promised to make a great nation through Abram (later God changed Abram's name to Abraham) and people of God.

2)   God promised to bless Abram including a long healthy life, wealth, and importance.

3)   Abraham's name would be remembered and honored in history.

4)   That Abraham would be a blessing by telling others about the living God.

5)   Those who blessed Abraham would be blessed.

6)   Those who cursed Abraham would be cursed.

7)   All families of the earth would be blessed.

Part of the sign of the covenant between God and Abraham can be found in Genesis 17:10-11, That the children would be circumcised and would be considered a part of the covenant. But those uncircumcised would not be considered part of the covenant.

In the book of Malachi 3:1-3, Malachi is prophesying of the coming of the Messiah. And Jesus will establish a new covenant between God and man. In v2 is about the second coming of Christ and purifying process and will sift through all people to prepare for His reign. If you go through the sifting process right now how would you come out? Would we be prepared? Just something to think about. The covenant is unchangeable. It is a solemn agreement with God made with us.

In (Job 31:1) [1] *I have made a covenant with my eyes. How could I gaze at a maid?* The covenant we make with God, should be taken very seriously. If Job could make a covenant with his eyes to not lust after other women, then why can't we make a covenant with ourselves to be Holy? Make a covenant with your hands not to touch anyone intimately until marriage, as God intended. Also, use our hands for things ordained by God, and set about the things He has put before you. Make a covenant with your mouth, not to say unkind or speak unjustly against one another. Make a covenant with your mind and keep it clean of evil thoughts and do not battle within your mind about your past. Leave it in the past. Make a covenant with your heart to love everyone, even the people you do not like or like the way they live. We still need to love them because that is Christ in us. That is the way He uses us to gain other's trust. Make a covenant to be truthful. People will trust you because you do not lie, and they will respect you. Make a covenant with your feet to go where God says go. By making a covenant with our bodies, then we can be faithful to our covenant with God and to that witness to fulfill the call on our lives. Keeping the covenant with our bodies, will always keep us consciously aware to keep the covenant with God and earn a reputation of integrity. When people come at us and accuse you, then you will be able to stand up to the attack, because you know the covenant you have made with yourself and God. God will be your defender and He will use the attack for His good and you will be stronger after coming through it with God's help. God will be there, and He will help you to shine in the end. The concept of the covenant goes so much deeper than just our bodies. The covenant can be applied in all areas in our lives. It should be put into operation in our church attendance, our tithing, our bill paying, and our jobs. God wants us to choose to glorify Him in everything, God made a covenant with us, to always look out for us, do what is best for us, to defend us, protect us, counsel us, and eventually take us home to be in His presence forevermore. He will always be faithful even when we falter in our covenant with Him. He loves His children beyond any word can describe. He will never give up on us.

If Christ came to earth in the flesh and at the same time be holy, then why can't we be in the flesh and be holy. Most people would respond by saying, because he was God and had all the power of God. We are God's people, and we are set apart by His forgiveness. When we became committed to Christ, we were set apart by His grace. We are called to be holy. Jesus was sinless and had the same emotions we have. He pooped in his diaper as a baby, just like we did. He had blood running His veins just like we do. And He bled just like we do. The difference is He was disciplined in His flesh. Do not misunderstand, He is to be revered and respected that He deserves, but we do need to identify on a personal level with Him. He understands us, knows what we face, because He faced the same things before being hung on a cross and resurrecting three days later.

The Hebrew meaning for discipline is reproof, is warning, restraint. There are many times we are going along in life and everything is going fine. Then we engage in unholy acts. The Holy Spirit tries to convince us to restrain ourselves, but we choose to ignore the Holy Spirits correction or discipline and plunge ahead anyway. God gave us free will to choose a life of holiness or a life of sin. God will gently correct us before we act on sin, but He will not force us to do the right thing. God is a gentleman; He will step back and wait until we come to our senses. He allows us to choose. (Proverbs 8:32-36) *³² Now therefore listen to me my children, for blessed are those who keep my ways. ³³ Hear the instructions and be wise and do not disdain it. ³⁴ Blessed is the man that heareth me, watching daily at my gates, waiting at the posts of my doors. ³⁵ For whosoever finds me finds Life and shall obtain favor of the Lord. ³⁶ But he that sins against me wrongs his own soul: all those hate me love death.* (Proverbs 4:13) *¹³ Take firm hold of instructions and do not let go. Keep her for she is your life.* When we receive the instructions of God and choose to listen to the corrections of the Holy Spirit and accept it, we receive wisdom, and the favor of God and a full life. We begin to discipline ourselves against sin. (Job 36:10-12) *¹⁰ He (the Holy Spirit) opens their ear to instruction and commands that they turn from their iniquity. ¹¹ If they obey and serve Him, they shall spend their days in prosperity and years in pleasures. ¹² But if they do not obey; they shall perish by the sword and they shall die without knowledge.* We know we need discipline over the flesh. How sad to die without the knowledge of the one who can give eternal life. Our jobs as Christians are more important now and becoming more urgent to spread the gospel as time goes on. There will come a day and time that we will not have any more time to perform the task that God has asked us to do. (Romans 8:1-4) *¹ There is therefore now no consideration to those who are in Christ Jesus who do not walk according to the flesh, but according to the Spirit. ² For the law of the Spirit of life in Christ Jesus has made me free from the law of sin and death. ³ For what the law could not do in that it was weak through the flesh, God did by sending His own son, in the likeness of sinful flesh on account of sin: He condemned sin in the flesh, ⁴ that the righteousness requirement of the law might be fulfilled in us who do not walk in the flesh, but according to the Spirit.* Look at these verses again. God sent His son in the likeness of sin in the flesh, because of sin to condemn sin. Jesus came as a representative of God, to show us the way of a full Spirit led life. We must remember that we too are representatives of God. (Genesis 1:26) *¹ Then God said let us make man in our image according to our likeness, let them have dominion over the fish of the sea, over the birds, and over the cattle, over all the earth, and over every creeping thing that creeps on the Earth.* As Representatives of God, we should set the higher standards as Christians for those not serving Christ. Dominion means to rule, exercise authority, lordship. We have the power over sin if we live by the power of the Spirit. (Romans 6:7-14) *⁷ For He who has died had been free form sin. ⁸ Now if we died with Christ; we believe that we shall also live with Him. ⁹ Knowing that Christ having been raised from the dead dies no more death, (sin) no longer has dominion over Him. ¹⁰ For death that He died, He died to sin once and for all, but the life that He lives He lives to God. ¹¹Likewise you also reckon yourselves to be dead indeed to sin, but alive to God in Christ Jesus our Lord. ¹² Therefore do not let sin reign in your mortal body, that you should obey it in its lusts. ¹³ And do not present your members as instruments of un-righteousness to sin but present yourselves to God as being alive form the dead and your members as instruments of righteousness to God. ¹⁴ For sin shall not have dominion over you, for you are not under law but grace.* (Read verse 11 again) When we made a commitment to live for God, SIN DIED. If sin died, then we have dominion of it because Christ gave us dominion. So, when we died to sin, we died to it once and for all. It is gone, not to be remembered anymore. When you have dominion over something, you have discipline that Christ had. God gave us dominion and discipline over sin by the death of Jesus. (1 Peter 1:13-21) *¹³Therefore gird up the loins of your mind, be sober, and rest your hope fully upon the grace that is to be brought you at the revelation of Jesus Christ. [14] as obedient children, not conforming yourselves to the former lusts, as in your ignorance, [15] but as He who called you is Holy, you also be holy in all your conduct, [16]because it is written, be holy for I am holy. [17] And if you call on the Father, who without, partiality judges according to each one's work, conduct yourselves throughout the time of your stay here in fear, [18] Knowing that you were not redeemed with the corruptible things, like silver or gold, from your aimless conduct received by tradition from your fathers, [19] but with the precious blood of Christ as of a lamb without blemish and without spot. [20] He indeed was forewarned before the foundation of the world, but was manifest in these last times for you, through Him who believe in God, who raised Him from the dead and gave Him glory, so that your faith and hope are in God.* We must redirect our thinking. We must make up our minds to resist temptation to sin. Holy means pure, morally blameless. When we are holy, we gain the respect of those living in the world. They begin to believe in Christ. They begin to see Him at work in us. We do not just say we live in Christ; we show them by our actions, the way we talk. The way we act, upholding godly appearances. They way we act in situations in our lives, reflect Christ in our lives. Relying on God in prayer to handle things for us, not telling everybody else and letting yourself be convinced to handle it yourself. (John 14:12) *[14] The works that I do you shall do also, and greater works than these shall he do because I go unto my Father.* (1 John 4:4) *[4] Greater is He who is in you than He who is in the world.* Most of us can quote these scriptures by heart, but do we believe them, apply them, and demonstrate it in our faith? God wants to bring restoration to His people and the way to do that, is to set ourselves apart and be holy, be disciplined and have the power over sin that God has given us. Act with authority of Christ when we are tempted. As we begin to use our faith. Power, and grace that God has given to us. He will begin to start working in us and through us in a mighty way. Search ourselves for anything that you are tempted by that you know if you give into that thing, it will cause you harm, mentally, physically, emotionally, and spiritually, and make a conscious decision to regain dominion over it. We must start training our minds to be holy, and then we will be what God wants us to be. Bottom Line: You are as holy as you want to be.

As Christians, we need to use the keys God gave us. We need to be what God has told us to be, a light in a world of darkness. We need to let His light shine and start standing up and saying no to the thing's society is trying to force upon us as acceptable. God does want to persevere and not give up. The biggest difference we can make is be about increasing the Kingdom of God, by telling others about Him and getting involved with the issue that are a part of society today, and let our actions be led by Christ. Let Christ help up to let the leaders know where we stand and what we want for our children, who are the future of the country. We need to get back to the Basic Biblical Principles of God and start upholding those principles in all aspects of our lives.

Chapter 6

Everywhere Else?

How many times do you say God bless you every day? How many times does a person sneeze, and you say bless you, but not God bless you? Even the simplest phrase has been compromised. How many times do we seek to encourage others to keep pressing on when life seems difficult? Are we allowing ourselves to be used by God? Are we sensitive to the Holy Spirit and listen when he prompts us to do something for someone, even when it requires a sacrifice on our part? Maybe we do not want to give or do what God has instructed us to do because of our own selfish reasons or fear of what others may think. If we are truly about God's business with a heart to serve and please God, then we need not worry, because He has His hand on it and the outcome. He will equip us with whatever it is we need to achieve His plan for our lives.

There is a story about how saying God bless you and prayer can touch a person's life that you do not even know.

Imagine a greeter, Sandy in a department store and she is really having a bad day, so much so that she does not even greet the shoppers as they come in and nobody notices until Cathy walks in, and she smiles at the greeter and says "Hello". Sandy replies with a mumbled "Hello". Cathy senses that something is going on in this young woman's life and stops and goes back to talk with the greeter. "I hope your day gets better and may God bless you". Sandy is surprised that this stranger seems to care that she is having a bad day. She feels so depressed and wishes she had someone to talk to. She thinks this person is probably just trying to be nice, but she gets another surprise. "May I pray for you?" Cathy asks Sandy. "I sure need it." Sandy replies.

Sandy begins to tell Cathy about her problems at home with her kids and how she is worried about them and how it is affecting her job. Cathy hugs Sandy and begins to fervently pray for God to make a difference in this young woman's life. When Cathy is through praying, Sandy can smile where she was not able to before.

For a few minutes prayer and a God bless you made a difference in someone's life. This really happened. My sister Cathy did stop and pray for this woman. I share this for the glory of God, to show his love. The greeters name is not really Sandy, to protect her privacy. We believe that her day went better, and that God did bless her and her children that day. When we use the keys given by God, we can help someone to begin to think about God and where He is in their lives and help them to see that He is there even when we are not seeking Him. A seed was planted that day and though Cathy may never see the fruits of that seed, God will continue to water it and help it to grow and send other people at the right times in that young woman's life to help her gain strength in her own faith in God and the good in people again.

That is God's love working. When you go to a store or a restaurant and say God bless you to the cashier, the waitress, or others around you, they will feel better. God will bless them because you asked Him to. If you believe in Jesus. It will also encourage you in knowing that you are doing what God has commanded. To go forth and show love for one another as He loved us.

(Psalms 115:12-13) *12 The Lord has been mindful of us. He will bless us. He will bless the house of Israel. He will bless the house of Aaron. 13 He will bless who fear the Lord both small and great.* We fall under this promise when we are a child of God because we are heirs to God's promises and His kingdom.

The greatest thing we can do is love, and love others. We need to humble ourselves and realize that we do not know everything and that we are not God. It is not about US! It is all about GOD!

We all get discouraged at times. We must be tested to strengthen our faith and belief in God, even in the hardest times. God is always there. He is just a prayer away. He hears every request. (Psalms 102:17) [17] *He shall regard your prayer of the destitute and shall not despise prayer.* Everything we ask God for, He will handle it, because He promised to do so. It does not always mean we get the answer we seek or that it will always be worked out how we imagined it, but God will always do what is right and better for our ultimate good. (John 15:16) [16] *You did not choose me, but I chose you and appointed you that you should go and bear fruit, and that your fruit should remain, that whatever you as the Father in My name, He may give you.*

God will lead you out of despair and give you hope. (1Corinthians 10:13) states that there is not a temptation that God will allow you to be tempted beyond what you are able to bear and that in that temptation, has already prepared a way out to escape that you will be able to bear it. God has plans for us and will put us where He wants us. God does not want us to be in evil things. God is love and peace. Seek Him in all things and the rest will take care of itself. When there are storms in your life, God is getting ready to promote you to the next level in your spiritual development. God will move in the storm and prepare us for work He has in store for us. In the midst of the storm, God will give you instruction on how to get through the storm, even its just to trust in Him. God will also keep His promise to bring you through the storm and remember every storm is a bridge to the supernatural. Listen and God's presence will be upon you.

Chapter 7
Facing God

In the end God will judge each and everyone. It is not our
place to judge others, because God has the final say, for He is
the ultimate judge. (Revelation 20:12-15)
   *¹² And I saw the dead small and great standing before God,
and the book was opened, which is the BOOK OF LIFE. And
the dead were judged according to their works, by the things
which were written in the books. ¹³ The sea gave up the dead
who were in it, and Death and Hade delivered up the dead who
were in them. And they were judged, each according to his
works.¹⁴ Then Death and Hades were cast into the lake of fire.
This is the second death. ¹⁵ And anyone not found written in the
Book of Life was cast into the lake of fire.*
      There are books that God keeps records of our lives in.
There is a book of remembrance. This book is used to record
every deed we have done in Christ's name. Every time we
meditate on God, seek God, Pray to God, Praise God, and
witness to someone else, it is being recorded. God also records
the deeds that we do that do not glorify Him. The ones we do
not repent of. Every believer's name is written in the Book Of
Life. And will be saved from Hell.

      We will stand before God and He will remind us of
everything. The Book of Life has the names of God's children
recorded in it. When we repent our names are entered in the
Book of Life and our deeds (sins) are remembered no more.
(Malachi3:16) *¹⁶ Then those who feared the Lord spoke to one
another, and the Lord listened and heard them; so a book of*

remembrance was written before him, for those who fear the Lord and who meditate on His name.

Jesus came to earth born of a virgin, Mary, performing miracles, He spent time with the lowliest of the lowly and lifted them up to see His greatness and showed them love, compassion, and mercy. He did not remind them of their sins, their faults, short comings. He still loves us. He gave His life, so that we could live. You can accept Him anytime and anywhere. Repent and tell Him you have sinned and ask Him to forgive those sins and to send His Holy Spirit to come and help you live for Him. Tell him that you relinquish control of your life to Him and you will have the promise of eternal life. Glory to God in the highest.

Made in the USA
Columbia, SC
29 October 2024

45019840R00030